Knowing Man

Knowing Man

(formerly, For Man's Sake!)

J. I. Packer, M.A., D.Phil.

Cornerstone Books
Westchester, Illinois

Contents

Preface

The first of these two pieces is an expanded and rewritten version of an address given in All Souls' Church, Langham Place, London in October 1977 at the first London rally of the Nationwide Festival of Light. Members of the Gay Christian Movement demonstrated at the rally, and it was not the easiest of situations in which to speak. I shall not soon forget the sensitive and to my eye inexpressibly sad faces of some of the "gays" who sat on the church carpet in front of me as I talked. It seemed clear to me that, as being a hippy is no guarantee of being happy, so being "gay" is no passport to gaiety, and some parts of my address were called forth on the spur of the moment by my desire to share the joy of knowing Christ with them particularly. I overran my time as a result, but still failed to say all I had intended. The additional material is inserted here, cast in the same rhetorical style as the rest.

The second piece was written in 1974 for a symposium produced by the Latimer House Church and Community Working Party under the title *Focus on Leviathan: Problem Areas for Christian Citizens.* The book failed to find a publisher and the authors have since cannibalized their chapters for use elsewhere. A shortened version of mine appeared in *Third Way* (April, 1977). Here it is revised and printed in full. It backs up some of the bolder generalizations which I have ventured to make in the address.

J. I. Packer

Part I: True Humanism

1
A Humanist Movement

I am a humanist. In truth, I believe it is only a thoroughgoing Christian who can ever have a right to that name. I am not the only one who believes this. In 1938 the Roman Catholic philosopher Jacques Maritain wrote a book calling for a reconstructed Christendom as our social target for tomorrow, and he boldly entitled his work *True Humanism.* More recently, we have seen the appearance in English of Hans Kung's 700-page treatise *On Being a Christian*, which is wholly devoted to spelling out and making good the claim that "Christianity cannot properly be understood except as radical humanism."[1] It would be well if Protestants took up this thesis more robustly, for it is true. It is part of the glory of the gospel to be the one genuine humanism that the world has seen.

What is humanism? Essentially, it is a quest: a quest for full realization of the possibilities of our humanity. We see ourselves as less satisfied, less fulfilled, less developed, less fully expressed, than we might be; we have not yet tasted all that could enrich us, nor yet developed all our creative potential, nor yet made the most of relationships with others, nor yet enjoyed all that is there to be enjoyed, nor yet fully harnessed the powers of the physical world as instruments of our freedom; and we long to enter further into what we see as our human heritage. In this basic sense we are all humanists; our natural self-love, which God implanted in us, makes us so. You would have to say of anyone who had ceased to look for personal enrichment in any of these ways (as alas, broken folk sometimes do) that he or she was hereby lapsing from one dimension of humanness, as if to contract out of the human race.

But some who claim to be humanists deny that Christians have any right to the title. I am thinking of those who call themselves secular, scientific, Marxist, or existentialist humanists. For the moment I shall not challenge their view of Christians; no doubt there are black spots in our record, and in our zeal for God's righteousness we have sometimes lost sight of basic human values, and the secular humanists are judging us as they find us. But I must tell you how their own claim to be humanists looks to me.

Please do not take offense at what I shall say now. I am not making a debating point, but spelling out in the fittest words I can find a conviction about humanness which for Christians is quite fundamental. What I have to say is this: they call themselves humanists; I think they are using the wrong word. The more exact name for their views would be brutism or animalism. Why? Because they tell us that the way to live is to turn our backs on God as Christians know him, to give up that ideal of the good life which the Bible and the Christian past bequeath to us, and to start "doing our own thing" without regard for any authority save the imperious promptings of our own hearts. Notwithstanding my deep respect for the integrity of those who take this line, I conceive that anyone who turns his back on God and God's revealed will for us forfeits a dimension of human dignity and settles for a way of life which in this respect befits the lower animals, but does not match the nature and potential of man at all.

Christian humanism of the evangelical type stands in the tradition of two other movements of the past, for both of which I heartily thank God—the Puritan movement of the seventeenth century, and the Methodist movement of the eighteenth. They too were humanist movements in the sense I have defined, and both had to face the same kind of flak from the uncomprehending and ill-disposed that comes the way of evangelical humanists today.

What sort of movements were Puritanism and Methodism? To describe either as a protest movement would be inadequate, though many gestures of protest issued from both. But whereas protest movements try to clear the ground of evil without taking responsibility for designing anything better to put in its place, Puritanism and Methodism were positive evangelical movements, attacking evils only in order to make room for the better things of the Christian gospel so that all life might become "holiness to the Lord." Similarly, to think of Puritanism or Methodism as Pharisaic would be a mistake. I would not blame anyone who had it in for Pharisaism, which is at motivational level an unlovely ego-trip compounded of pride and envy. But though Puritans and Methodists were accused of spiritual pride in their own day and later, the accusation will not stick, save perhaps to substandard specimens of each kind. The zeal for God's praise which animated Puritans and Methodists was a different thing from Pharisaic self-righteousness.

Nor, finally, was either Puritanism or Methodism a kill-joy movement. I know they are often thought of in those terms, Puritanism in particular, but this is lampooning them. Thus, for example, Shakespeare in *Twelfth Night* had Sir Toby Belch describe the odious kill-joy Malvolio ("ill-wisher" is what his name means) as "a kind of Puritan"; Lord Macaulay said that the Puritans hated bearbaiting not because it gave pain to the bear but because it gave pleasure to the spectators; H. L. Mencken defined Puritanism as the fear that somewhere, somehow, someone is enjoying himself; and John Mortimer, Q.C., who so often appears for the defense these days in obscenity trials, has recently gone on record as saying, "I think there is a tremendously strong streak of Puritanism in the English national make-up that we must guard against."[2]

The stereotype of Puritanism which these remarks reflect is of a negative, morose repressiveness, culturally impoverishing, but this is historically a complete mistake. What the Puritans opposed was not fun and games as such, but fun and games of a demoralizing and dehumanizing type. Thus, they opposed, not alcohol or sex, but drunkenness and debauchery. Thus, they closed theaters, not because they were against drama as such (some were, but only a minority), but because theaters were centers of prostitution.

Similarly, John Wesley taught the Methodists to have nothing to do with brutalizing amusements like cockfighting and bearbaiting, which were still going on in England. Wesley has been criticized for this, as if he too belonged to the genus kill-joy. But Wesley, the man who once said that there is no Christianity but social Christianity and no holiness but social holiness, was trying to clear a place in men's lives for the joy of the Lord. It was noticed that under the teaching of this supposed kill-joy folk learned to sing at their work, just as Wesley himself loved to sing as he rode from place to place to preach the gospel. To sing! Yes, for something had happened to them. They had found God through Jesus Christ, and joy had come pouring in.

What about evangelical Christian humanism today? Surely it is no more a protest movement, or a Pharisaic movement, or a kill-joy movement, than were Puritanism and Methodism. Nor is it a mere outburst of social conservatism, a flight by the middle-aged of the middle class back from the present into the womb of the past, to the manners and customs of the days we would refer to by the phrase, "when I was young. . ." What is it, then? The answer seems to be: it is a movement raised up by God for cleaning up moral messes in our society. Ways and styles of life which tend to coarsen, brutalize and dehumanize, undermining human dignity by encouraging us irresponsibly to follow instinct, like animals ("if it feels good, do it"), are widely adopted and promoted today. Evangelical Christian humanism challenges these because they keep folk from the true fullness and joy of human life under God. The purpose of the challenge is not simply to get rid of things which hurt man and dishonor God, but primarily to create space for the gospel. As an involved observer of this movement, it seems clear to me that this is essentially what it is about.

2

A Vision of Humanness

Now let me share with you more fully my own vision and ideal of achieved humanness, the vision which I find evangelical Christian humanism embracing just as the Puritans and Wesley did in earlier days. I realize that I can only do this here in formulary terms, but I hope that even the sketchiest mental framework will be better than nothing at all, and of course we can all work privately at filling it in after the meeting is over! So I offer you this formula, which I believe crystallizes a great deal that is in the Bible. Humanness, the natural expression and fulfilment of the nature our Maker gave us, consists of *a life-pattern of relationships in which God is adored and his image in us is fulfilled.*

This formula, as you see, assumes three things: first, that relationships are of the essence of our life; second, that worship of God is natural to us, and necessary for our per-

sonal well-being; third, that as purposive action resulting in personal change is the shape
of all our conscious living, so God's image
must be thought of not just as something
static and given, like a tattoo that stays on me
whether I like it or not, but also as a condi-
tion which is more or less achieved according
to how I use my God-given capacities. The
given capacities (the image viewed formally)
are powers of thought, of construction, of
management, of moral discernment and of re-
lating responsively to other rational beings.
The fulfilment of the image (the image
viewed substantially) consists of actual rationality, creativity, mastery of environment,
righteousness and community. The first and
second of these assumptions I must take for
granted now (they would not, I think, be
hard to defend if challenged); the third however needs to be spelled out.

Where do we learn of God's image in man?
In the first chapter of Genesis, where, as the
climax of the story of how God shaped up the
glorious complexities of the natural order, we
read this: "And God said, Let us make man
in our image, after our likeness"—the two
phrases mean the same—"and let them have
dominion . . . over all the earth. . . . So God
created man in his own image; in the image
of God created he him"—the repetition is for

emphasis—"male and female created he them" (Genesis 1:26-7; cf. 9:6; James 3:9). We need not look outside Genesis 1 to find the five items which, as I urged above, combine to make up God's image in man, both as an endowment and as an achievement. Here they are.

First comes *rationality*, the gift of intelligence and the power to reason and make plans. Creation, as depicted in Genesis 1, was the work of a mighty mind, forming and executing purposes ("Let there be . . .") and then evaluating its own achievement ("God saw everything that he had made, and behold it was very good"). God made man in his own image to have dominion over the earth and all its contents: reason, on the pattern if not with the power of God's reason, was needed for that, just as man needed reason if God was to be able to address him in words. Man could not know, love or serve God without this endowment of reason with which to apprehend him. Rationality is thus the basic element in God's image, and is presupposed in fact by each of the other four items in it which we are to look at now.

Second comes *creativity*, the capacity to make things and thereby impart value to them. It is good that in this twentieth century, when for so many daily work has be-

come a monotonous drudgery, we are at last
starting to appreciate the preciousness of our
natural creativity, and the importance of
exercising it if we are to live full-orbed and
contented lives. In Genesis 1 God appears as
the great Creator; this fact about him fills the
whole of verses 1-25; so that when he says,
"Let us make man in our image," we are evidently meant to understand that God intends
man, within his limits, to be a creator too.

It is man's privilege and joy under God to
be artist and craftsman, producing as God
did things that are good and have value. I, for
instance, am a writer; I create books. I work
hard at them, I put a lot of myself into them,
and I get much joy from finding, as I sometimes do, that what I slogged away at now
has value for somebody. Again, a home-
maker puts her heart and her back into creating a place to live that is beautiful, comfortable and welcoming, and finds joy when her
family and friends appreciate the value of
what she has done. Again, married couples
make babies; God gives them the thrilling
though awesome privilege of creating new
human life, and of molding and shaping the
children's growth by the way they bring
them up. Arts and crafts, performing skills,
homemaking, family life—these are all
spheres of creativity, in which this aspect of

God's image in us is expressed and displayed.

Third comes *dominion,* mastery over created things. We read that when God resolved to create man in his image he said: "and let them have dominion." God made us with the intention that we should control our environment by harnessing and managing the forces of nature; thus our lives become an image of God's own lordship over all things. This amounts to saying that God summons men to create a culture, a civilization, in which through cooperation one with another life is made richer than otherwise it could be. The fantastic technological advances of our time enable us to go further in doing this than any previous generation could.

Technology is not intrinsically sinful or soulless. Granted, technology is often used sinfully and soullessly to gain wealth and power at others' expense, and our duty to be good stewards of God's precious creation, not raping and ruining it by wanton squandering of natural resources, is often disregarded. But that does not mean that technology is evil in itself, only that it is being misdirected and mishandled. "Let them have dominion" is in effect God's directive to us to develop a technology as a means of mastery.

The Creator is glorified when the possibilities of his creation are realized and developed by human enterprise, provided that this is done responsibly, in a way that benefits others. Recognition of our responsibility to use created things for the Creator's praise may be a rare thing in our time, yet dominion remains an abiding element of the image of God in human life.

Fourth in the list comes *righteousness*, by which I mean the doing of God's revealed will, so that our lives embody his moral preferences and make for his pleasure. We read that once God had made men he gave them their orders: "God blessed them, and God said to them, Be fruitful and multiply, and fill the earth and subdue it; and have dominion . . ." (Gen. 1:28). The essence of righteousness is to obey God's orders and do what he says, for the will of our morally perfect God is the rule of what is right for us, his creatures. The Bible has a name for God's teaching on how we should live: the name is *law*, in Hebrew *torah*.

The biblical idea of God's law is not, in the first instance, that of a public legal code (though God gave Israel its public legal code), but of friendly authoritative instruction such as a wise father gives his children. That is what *torah* means. God's law is his kindly word to us as our Creator who cares for us and wants to lead us into rewarding paths. To be sure, disobedience to God's law will bring retribution, but the law was given not primarily to threaten us, rather to guide us into what is good for us. If God's law becomes a threat to us, that is because of our own negative and defiant attitude to it, just as civil laws protecting property, which are beneficial in themselves, become a threat to anyone who decides to become a burglar. What God commands is in fact no less good for us than it is pleasing to him; for the righteousness that he requires fits our human nature as our shoes fit our feet.

In these days in which we let ourselves be led so largely by the hunting and herd instincts of the jungle, and are reluctant to acknowledge any law save that of urges welling up from the depths of our fallen nature, it is well to be reminded that God's revealed law stands related to us human beings as the owner's manual stands related to our cars. You need not read the manual, or take any notice of what it says—but you can expect your car to give trouble if you handle it differently from the way the manual directs. And we can expect our human nature, which was designed to operate in obedience to God's law and experience freedom and fulfilment, contentment and joy in so doing, to give a vast amount of trouble if we break the bounds and use or, rather, misuse our humanity in a different way.

Think about sex, now, in the light of that last statement. This is an age of frank talk about sex: let me do a little frank talking on my own account. A moment ago we recalled God's command to man to subdue the earth. Note, however, that this was only the second thing God told man to do to the earth; his first appointed task was to be fruitful, and multiply, and fill it. But if procreation is commanded, then sexual relations are commanded, and sex is among other things fun.

Can it be that God actually commands us to have fun? Surely not, says somebody; at least, not that much fun! No, you are wrong. You are in good company, I grant you; the great St. Augustine, chief post-apostolic architect of all Western Christianity, held that sex within marriage for affection, affirmation, tenderness and pleasure, as distinct from the holy purpose of procreation, could never be quite right, and many noble souls since his day have swallowed this bitter teaching without a murmur. But by biblical standards Augustine was wrong, just as you are.

Look at the Song of Solomon—a canonical love lyric! Certainly, it is there to picture the

Lord's love for his people, but that does not alter the fact that it is the duet of a committed and faithful human couple celebrating their mutual attraction and affection. And look at Proverbs 5:18-19 (RSV): "Rejoice in the wife of your youth . . . let her affection fill you at all times with delight, be infatuated always with her love." There can be no doubt about it: when God told the man and the woman to multiply, he was telling them, and intending them, to have fun. For married couples, the joy of sex is commanded by God.

C. S. Lewis's Screwtape disgustedly called the Creator "a hedonist at heart," because he wants to see us happy and loves to make us so. No doubt God's direction of married persons into the pleasure of sexual love was one thing Screwtape had in mind. When in 1949 the Pope asked Louis Armstrong whether he had any children, the Baptist jazzman replied, "Not yet, but we're having a lot of fun trying." Armstrong's statement, though perhaps unexpected, was from a Christian standpoint entirely proper, as was the good laugh with which the Pope greeted it.[3]

There is, of course, another side to this coin. The Bible sets strict bounds to our use of our sexual powers. Relationships are to be heterosexual only, and limited to couples with a lifelong mutual commitment, and not planned in terms of a permanent refusal to procreate. Fornication, adultery and homosexual intercourse are ruled out, and it is made clear that the full God-intended joy (which is much more than the physical kick) will not be found along those paths. Abstinence within marriage will be right on occasion (1 Cor. 7:5), and virginity is the appropriate way of life for some. Jesus, who said this (Matt. 19:10-12), was himself an instance of it, and it would be hard to maintain that his humanity, or that of Jeremiah, who was told not to marry (Jer. 16:2), or that of Paul, who, whether a widower or deserted by his wife after his conversion, had no sexual partner throughout his ministry, was thereby diminished.

The standards of sexual self-control for all and sexual abstinence for some are explicit, and here as everywhere grace to live by God's standards will be given to all who seek it. Just as there is joy and fulfilment in using sex responsibly within marriage, so there is joy and fulfilment in obediently restraining sex outside marriage, both of which things God can enable us to do. And life's deepest joy will always be found in doing what we know to be God's will.

Now what is true of sex, the subject matter

of God's first command to man in Genesis 1, is true of all divine commands. Sex is a paradigm case, a clear example of what is true of God's law in every sphere of life. Disregard it, affirming against it your own autonomy, and the result is strain and distress deep down, because in addition to displeasing God you do violence to your own nature. Keep the law, and in thus serving God you find freedom and delight, because human nature is programmed for fulfilment through obedience.

Deliberate doing of God's will is man's only truly natural way of living. As there are natural and unnatural eating habits, so there are natural and unnatural moral habits, and all defiance of divine law is unnatural and does us damage. You don't believe me? Well, I can understand that. One effect of the distorting twist called sin which the Bible diagnoses in all of us is to make it our habit not to believe what God says. More fools we!—for our disbelief does not make it untrue, and if we will not take God's words as our steppingstones to walk by they will become our stumbling blocks, over which we trip and fall.

Righteousness, then, meaning obedience to God's revealed will both in procreation and in all else, is the crucial and joyous fourth element in the image of God which we were all of us made to bear.

Fifth and last comes *community*, or togetherness. God made us to live in society— as John Donne said, no man is an island. Life is relationships, and we can only live fully human lives in fellowship with other people, in family, church, civil community, clubs, friendships and so on. Is this togetherness an aspect of the divine image? There are good grounds for saying, yes. Did you notice the plural pronouns in God's decision recorded in Genesis 1:26, "Let *us* make man in *our* image"? It is not the "us" of royalty or authorship (Hebrew knows neither of these idioms); it is the "us" of plurality. Here as elsewhere Hebrew, which has no lack of singular words for God, denotes him by a word with a plural form, and by plural pronouns. Why?

Christians down the ages have seen this plural as a hint—no more, but equally no less—of the personal plurality in God which becomes explicit in the New Testament disclosure of the Trinity. God, we now know, is intrinsically a society; provided you do not go over the edge into tritheism, you could even call him, as has been done, a corporation, Father, Son and Holy Spirit. (I am reminded of the printing at the top of an envelope that once came to me from the U.S.A.: *God and Son Inc., Doing Business for 2000 years with Sinners Like You.*) So it seems right to say that the togetherness which is essential to our well-being as persons is actually a further item in the image of God which we are called to reflect and embody in our life activities.

If, now, God's image in man consists, as we have urged, in the combination of rationality, creativity, mastery, obedience to God and community, which means togetherness with others, and if it is true that we were created with all these capacities so that we might actualize them in daily life, then we can see at once what a genuinely human life style will be like. It will unite worship with work, and responsible planning with creative use of created things; it will be marked by grateful and caring dependence on our family and friends and outgoing service of others, a Samaritanship shaped by the particular needs, material and spiritual, by which we find our neighbor beset. (Neighborliness, as the Good Samaritan story reveals it, goes as wide as need, and so can include both public and social service, such as Joseph and Daniel rendered in pagan governments, and personal spiritual ministry, such as Paul the missionary fulfilled to his converts.)

Such is the way of living for which God planned us, and only such living fulfils the deepest instincts of our nature. (Note, please, that I said *nature*, not *body*; the instincts of our nature go beyond, and are more basic than, the drives of our body.) Only such living as is described, therefore, realizes the dignity of human life and brings fulfilment to the human individual. Thus only this kind of living is truly natural. It is a mark of our sophisticated age to pine for what is natural—natural childbirth, natural food-stuffs and feeding habits, natural sound, or whatever. If we would also embrace God's teaching on the life style that is natural for us, what gain it would be!

3

Godliness and Humanness

The vision of life that I am spelling out has religion built into it, and not in any superficial way either. There is an important point here. Most people seem to think of religion—the worship of God, the acknowledging of his law, the pursuit of personal holiness and the service of others for God's sake as well as theirs—as if it were an extra to be added to behavior patterns which have found their basic shape already: icing on the cake of life, so to speak, one more enriching interest to add to the many one already has.

This view fits in with—indeed, grows out of—the modern secular view of religion as a private and personal hobby, and no doubt the invitation to accept Christ and become a Christian is sometimes understood in this way, but we ought not to think in such terms, for they falsify the whole situation. All our life at every point is being lived unnaturally if God is not at the center, and if his praise and glory ("hallowed be thy name") is not the supreme concern throughout. Do let us be clear on that.

I said a moment ago that a great dehumanizing infection has attacked all our lives, the motivational twist called sin, a hidden force working away in the human heart much as the beetles work away under the bark of trees with Dutch Elm disease, and with comparable killing effect. Sin perverts instincts not only in our bodies but also, more fundamentally, in our natures, and leads us to turn our backs on God, go our own way, do our own thing, live for ourselves, realize Satan's image in our life style instead of God's, and then turn around and challenge Christian ideals as antihuman, bigoted and pathetic.

I know, indeed, that some who take this line are the embittered victims of insensitive and loveless treatment which has claimed, in a manner reminiscent of Dickens's more nauseous hypocrites, to be Christianly motivated, and I hope you will believe me when I say I grieve for these folk and am heartily ashamed of what professed Christians have said and done to them. But you will have observed, as I have, that the thinking of a sensitive person who has been deeply hurt will thereafter be shaped by reaction against that which damaged him, and he will not therefore be free at that point to think straight.

But the deeper truth is that sin within us allures us all into anti-God ways of behavior, feeling and thought, of which skepticism about God's teaching given us in the Bible is one sign. If you find yourself incredulous when I tell you that the life I have pictured is the good life for us all, and that God tells us so and Christian experience over and over again has proved it so, I can well understand it: your attitude reveals that sin has got at your mind, as part of its assault on your heart, and I can only implore you to fight sin in your mind, and think again, and challenge your own unbelief, and be skeptical about your skepticism. God knows, we live in days when it is hard to fight the invading flood of unbelief, but I challenge anyone to produce better *reasons* for regarding the anti-God way, rather than the way of godliness, as the good life for you and me.

I hope that by saying these things I help you to see the law of God in its true light. That law is not a straightjacket, imposing on us arbitrary and unnatural limitations and so making life poor, but the liberating and enriching directive for integrated and joyous human fulfilment. What blossoms from the seeds of self-discipline which God's law seeks to plant within us is, quite simply, a deeper delight than otherwise we shall ever know. Can you believe it? I hope you can, for tens of thousands of folk today could stand up and assure you from personal experience that it is so. And I hope that our line of thought will help you to understand the gospel in its true light also, as you see how it subserves God's beneficent law.

You ask me: what is the gospel? I reply: it is Jesus Christ, the crucified Savior and risen Lord. It is not just the truth about him; it is Jesus himself, who comes to us and speaks to us in person through the truth that Scripture and Christians tell us about him. Really and truly, though of course invisibly, he draws near to us in the power of his deity, his atoning death, his risen life and his present heavenly reign, and says to us what he has always said to sinners: "Come to me, all you who are under strain and find life burdensome, and I will give you rest. I'll give you peace for your guilty conscience, the peace of pardon and a restored relationship with God, and where your life is muddled and twisted and astray, I'll sort you out and set you on the right track. Learn from me; my yoke is easy, and the demands of discipleship that I shall lay upon you, which now perhaps scare you stiff in prospect, will not crush you as you fear.''[4] If you hear his word and turn to him in sincerity, that is precisely what will happen, and how you will find things to be.

But how does the Savior sort us out and set us straight? What he does in effect is to take us to the law, and then say: ''Now look at me. The law spells out true humanness verbally; I have lived it out practically. See me, if you will, as the law incarnate, just as I am God's grace incarnate, and understand that law keeping in imitation of me is the pattern of life into which I am now leading you.'' ''But it's too hard for me,'' you object. ''All right,'' says the Savior in effect, ''so it is; I knew that, and have made provision for it. I send upon you the Holy Spirit. What you cannot do in your own strength you will be able to do in his. Now let me lead you in the power of the Spirit to adopt, for the first time in your life, a fully human way of living, and let me prove to you that the joy and contentment which the self-denying Christian knows is far beyond anything that the self-indulgent pagan has ever conceived.''

What we have to appreciate is that Christ saves us from the guilt and alienation of sin in order then to free us from its dominion on a day-to-day basis, so that we actually keep the law. We were made to keep it, and we are redeemed to keep it. This is the way of godliness, which is also the way of humanness. I hope you can see it, and that your heart tells you even now that by God's grace you are actually on it.

4
Drifting into Godlessness

The streams of Western culture are flowing away from godliness. Society is being increasingly secularized: that is, it is undergoing the change which sociologists call secularization, and define as transition from a state in which religious faith shaped community life to one in which religion is just a private hobby for minority interest groups, and community life is controlled by nonreligious considerations. Take my country, for example. Whereas nineteenth-century England was Christian, not indeed always in achievement (horrible things were done), but certainly in intention and public commitment, twentieth-century England, despite Christian forces still operating in national life, is plainly anxious to be a secular rather than a Christian country. What have I to say about that?

Quietly and calmly (for hysteria here does not help) I want to say two things.

First, this drift into secularism was inevitable. Why? Because in the thinking of so many major philosophers, and latterly of artists, historians, social scientists and professional communicators too, God has shrunk to such tiny proportions—almost to vanishing point. No longer are men aware of him as the mighty, worshipful Lord of the Old and New Testaments and of such epochs of faith as the sixteenth-century Reformation, the seventeenth-century Puritan period, and the Evangelical Revival of the eighteenth century. God has been so thoroughly reduced in size by these thinkers, and their impact on our culture has been so great, that many who see themselves as his servants no longer think of him as ruling his world in providence, or speaking to men in Holy Scripture, or even as being a personal moral being as opposed to an animating cosmic force.

To be sure, any who worship Jesus as Son of God incarnate, come to save the world, have in their beliefs about him an answer to all this. The fulfilling of prophecy in Jesus' life and death, and the achieving of the world's predestined redemption through the apparent accident of a Roman governor being willing to let justice miscarry in order to avoid trouble, prove clearly enough the reality of God's overruling. The fact that the second person of the Godhead became a teacher in Palestine settles the much-debated question whether God gives man verbal instruction. The fact that God incarnate has for nineteen centuries appeared unique among men in both the force of his personality and the moral grandeur of his life and teaching sinks all doubts as to whether God is personal or moral. But clearheaded and thoroughgoing believers are, it seems, a minority, and we should not wonder that when, on top of the work of the God-shrinkers, the knowledge and technology explosions of our time hit us, great numbers of folk were swept away from their Christian moorings altogether.

Some of us remain cultural dinosaurs, still acknowledging the God of the Bible, and believing that the Bible is his Word and Jesus Christ is his Son. Can such old-fashioned beliefs be true? Yes, I think so, but they are certainly not fashionable. Yet now, living as we do in a situation in which the pendulum has swung away from Christianity, there is need to take some action to try to reverse the swing; otherwise, those around us will never know the one and only formula for true humanness. It is no love of our neighbor to keep that concealed from him, little as he may want to hear it.

Second, the current drift into secularism is

impoverishing. The Christian tide has gone out, leaving behind it the spiritual equivalent of mud. Three aspects of this sad and unsightly mess call for particular mention.

The going out of the Christian tide has left behind it a world of *misunderstanding*. Men misunderstand themselves. The human being has always been a problem to himself. He is, and in lucid moments knows that he is, half ape and half angel, a kind of cosmic amphibian, grand in his powers, pathetic often in his performance. Says Shakespeare's Hamlet: "What a piece of work is man! How noble in reason! How infinite in faculty [capacity]! in form, in moving, how express and admirable! in action how like an angel! in apprehension how like a god! the beauty of the world! the paragon of animals!"

Hamlet is right: do we realize, I wonder, the fantastic glory of our humanity?

But what can man today do when he has given up on God, closed his Bible, and so lost the clue to a truly human way of living? What we do in fact is oscillate. We swing between aspiring to be like angels and consenting to act like apes. That is what is happening in our society: that is what so-called "permissiveness" is about: folk think the way of happiness is to combine idealism with self-indulgence, high-minded altruism with callous sensuality. But this is to misunderstand ourselves utterly.

The truth is that because we have lost touch with God and his word we have lost the secret both of community (because sin kills neighbor-love) and of our own identity (because at the deepest level we do not know who or what we are, or what we exist for). And only when we have relearned our identity as God's sinning and straying creatures, and, in the words of the hymn, "heard the voice of Jesus say, 'Come unto me and rest,' " can we hope to find a satisfactory way of living either with ourselves or with each other. And only then shall we find the deepest of all life's secrets—the secret of *contentment*.

What does it mean to be content? Contentment, which is directly bound up with happiness, fulfilment and joy, the realities of which I have been speaking, means this: unwillingness to change your lot for all the tea in China or the gold in Fort Knox (or wherever the gold is kept nowadays), because you are conscious of having found and of already enjoying life's best—that which of all things is most precious and delightful. The contented man knows that he has found the pearl of great price and secured the hidden treasure, and that there is nothing better, so he declines to consider exchanging it. One does not exchange the best for something less good.

Now in this sense the Christian is content, for in living with God as his Father and Jesus Christ as his Savior he knows a peace within that is to him more precious than anything else has ever been, and he knows too that he is heir to all the delight he can hold both now and for eternity. But where man's nature is not understood in terms of his relationship with God and his need to be forgiven and changed by grace, such contentment as this can never be known, and we are doomed to continue restless, always seeking something more than we have and never finding what in our hearts we crave for.

5

The Wasteland

Then again, the going out of the Christian tide has left behind it a world of *mirages*. Pardon the mixture of metaphors, but "mirages" is the notion I need here. A mirage is the appearance of an oasis in the desert. The parched traveller takes heart when he sees it and plods groggily towards it, longing for water to relieve his thirst; but he finds there is nothing there. The mirage deludes, and so do the alternative prospects of human fulfilment to which men turn when they abandon Christianity.

Some today, for instance, embrace *utopianism*, the hope of achieving a perfect society, whether by social evolution, such as Western liberals envisage, or by social revolution such as card-carrying Communists anticipate and work for. Without disrespect to the integrity of utopians, I have to say that George Orwell's *Animal Farm* and *1984* (which I urge you to read, if you have not already done so) really do seem to speak the last word as to what must happen when in a technological age an attempt is made to implement a utopian program. Power, which was used for selfish and brutal purposes before, may change hands, but after that it inevitably comes to be used for selfish and brutal purposes again. Power still corrupts, and absolute power still corrupts absolutely, and in that respect there is nothing new under the sun.

Others turn to *aestheticism*, that is, the policy of enlarging individual experience, maximizing sensation and tasting as many different activities and feelings as you can, in the belief that this is the way of happiness. It boils down to the maxim of Jerry Rubin the hippy: "If it feels good, do it." So we live life as a series of trips, some hectic, some relaxed, some planned, some on the spur of the moment, some with drink, some with drugs, some heterosexual, some homosexual, and so on. We join the aesthetic jet set, zooming from one expected pleasure (or should I say, antidote to boredom, or psychic pain-killer?) to another.

The formula sounds magically good; but what happens? Bitter experience confirms what has already been said—that you can fill your life with kicks of all sorts without fulfilling your nature or enlarging your joy in the least. Indeed, it is one of life's sad paradoxes, which aestheticists verify constantly, that by increasing the number and variety of pleasures you may actually decrease joy. Poor pathetic Marie Antoinette had everything a queen could ask for, and ended up bored stiff: her final complaint was, *"Nothing tastes."* Pleasure seeking, of whatever kind and at whatever level, is subject to the law of diminishing returns. The heartache of inner emptiness becomes more acute, and no contentment is found at all.

Can you see this? Can you distinguish between pleasure and joy? I hope so; you will not know what to do with your life otherwise. Joy brings contentment, pleasures as such don't, but joy makes life a pleasure even without those particular pleasures for which we might be tempted to envy others—such is the truth we need to guide us; but these are lessons which aestheticism forbids us to learn. The mirage presents itself as reality, the lie as truth, and many, one fears, are fooled.

Some who have seen through both utopianism and aestheticism settle for *pessimism*, which is in fact the only coherent possibility that remains when Christianity is given up. Human dignity, it is suggested, requires us to face the fact that there is no real hope for either the individual or society, and to be brave about it. Joy and fulfilment, in the sense in which we have been speaking of them, are themselves a mirage; there is really no such thing; it is not that we have lost the key of the door, but rather that there never was a door there.

In our time, anti-Christians like the late Bertrand Russell have settled for this kind of pessimism, and one cannot but admire their integrity and strength of will in doing so. But their view itself, so far from being a modern novelty, is in fact no more than a reviving of what the best philosophers, Stoic and Epicurean, were saying in the first century A.D., when Christianity was born. Life, they said, is inherently painful; the wise man's wisdom is to cut pain down to the minimum; that is the best we can ever hope to do. So the Epicureans counselled quiet retirement, and the Stoics taught men to be unfeeling in order to reduce their emotional vulnerability, and both agreed that the best option would certainly on occasion be suicide.

Similar pessimism permeates Eastern religion, which tells us that the best we can hope for is to come off the wheel of reincarnation and cease to exist personally at all. At the heart of pessimism is often the destructive reaction of hurt pride, the feeling that, having been disillusioned and let down by the optimists, one owes it to oneself to deny and try now to smash the hopes they entertain. It is like a person denouncing marriage as an evil because his own marriage has come to grief. But whatever the motivation, however murky and unreasonable it may be, pessimism itself is deeply tragic, for the state of hopelessness is in truth an antechamber of both death and hell.

Such, then, are the false hopes and the false denial of hope which we see growing like weeds in the wasteland of our present-day society.

Lastly, the going out of the Christian tide has left behind it a world of *menace*. The social discipline which Christian faith created and undergirded in the West is crumbling away into post-Christian indiscipline and disorder. Our heritage of Christian moral capital is shrinking, and some day we may wake up to find it all effectively gone. The peculiar hardness and frenzy which marks individual apostates from Christian faith has its counterpart in apostate societies, which achieve their paganism by directly rejecting a Christian heritage.

O. R. Johnston has written of *Christianity in*

a Collapsing Culture.[5] It would be hard to dismiss as unwarranted the judgment on our era which his title embodies. It is true that Britain today publicly purposes to be caring and compassionate in the same way that a century ago Britain publicly purposed to be Christian, but the steady increase in Britain of lawlessness, violence and anarchic self-indulgence, along with the weakening of home and family life and the breakup of social and economic restraints that operated before, are facts which will not go away, however much we act the ostrich and hide our eyes.

Yet the same realism which prompts initial alarm requires us also to note that for the moment British national life is on a kind of moral plateau. We are no longer publicly pro-Christian, but we are not yet publicly anti-Christian either. Though the boat has shipped a dangerous amount of water, it is not yet certain to sink. The law and the media still do as much to conserve the old values as they do to undermine them. The situation still allows Christians to act with some hope of arresting the anti-Christian pendulum-swing of our time.

6
Counterattack

But what can Christians do? What should they be trying to do? Answering with headings only (for space precludes anything more), I reply: we must aim, with God's help, to do four things together.

First, *recover vision*, the vision of true humanness under God, the goal towards which Christian action in society must always be directed.

Second, *restore concern*, and avoid the tolerance trap, by which I mean willingness to tolerate the intolerable. I know that tolerant inaction is a prime virtue in a permissive society, but I also know that all that is needed for evil to triumph in any human situation is for good men to do nothing. You know that too.

Third, *renew evangelism*, making it our top priority to win our fellow men and women to faith in Christ.

Fourth, *rebuild community*, at home in the family and abroad in society, so creating a milieu which helps on the human maturity that flows from Christian faith.

Some sentences from Nehemiah's narrative of the rebuilding of ruined Jerusalem say what we all need to hear as we contemplate this daunting task.

Sanballat and Tobiah . . . plotted together to come and fight against Jerusalem and to cause confusion in it. And we prayed to our God, and set a guard as a protection against them day and night. . . .

I looked, and arose, and said to the nobles and to the officials and to the rest of the people, "Do not be afraid of them. Remember the Lord, who is great and terrible, and fight for your brethren, and your sons, your daughters, your wives, and your homes."

I said to the nobles and to the officials and to the rest of the people, "The work is great and widely spread, and we are separated. . . . In the place where you hear the sound of the trumpet, rally to us there. Our God will fight for us" (Nehemiah 4:7 f., 14, 19 f.).

Amen.

Notes
[1]Hans Kung, *On Being a Christian* (London: Collins, 1977), p. 31.
[2]*Time*, August 22, 1977, p. 5.

[3]Max Jones and John Chilton, *Louis* (St. Albans: Mayflower, 1975), p. 226.

[4]Cf. Matthew 11:28-30. The Prayer Book Communion Service introduces verse 28 with the invitation: "Hear what comfortable words our Saviour Christ saith unto all that truly turn to him."

[5]Exeter: The Paternoster Press, 1976.

Part II: Secularism

7

What Is Secularization?

Sociologically, the standard definition of secularization is, as Bryan Wilson frames it, "the process whereby religious thinking, practice and institutions lose social significance"[1]— the process, that is, whereby the various spheres of community life are "desacralized" through being transferred from religious control based on transcendent, "other-worldly" sanctions to some sort of technological control based on the belief that life in this world will hereby be made better. For what the process of secularization expresses is not in the first instance skepticism about traditional religion (though this may be, and often is, part of it); the first thing it expresses is a shift of the community's ruling interest from the possibilities of the next world to the possibilities of this one.

What prompts the shift is the discovery that technology can sweeten and transform human circumstances in a way that earlier ages never dreamed of. Such a shift could happen anywhere, and is currently happening almost everywhere. Thus, for instance, in India, where for centuries British judges conscientiously preserved and administered Hindu and Muslim law, the independent Republic has decided (I quote Lesslie Newbigin, sometime Bishop of Madras) "that India shall be a secular state dedicated to the achievement of a socialist pattern of society . . . legislation . . . is determined by the intention that every citizen, irrespective of his religion or lack of it, shall be able to participate in the benefits and responsibilities of a welfare state. Thus legislation has been passed which is aimed to destroy completely elements in traditional religious law which are considered incompatible with this intention, such as untouchability, the dowry system and so on. These legislative acts, while they certainly lead public practice rather than following it, express the change which has in fact taken place in the way that Indians think about life."[2]

So it is not only in England, nor only in countries where Christianity has been dominant, that the forces of urbanization and industrialization, egged on by desire for overall material betterment, have snapped the strings by which a "sacral" society—that is, a community whose life was determined and interpreted by a religion—was previously held. Indeed, it is arguable that English secularization is mild compared with what happened in some places, for whatever else current legislation is doing it is not outlawing any part of Christian practice—not yet, at any rate. And this may alert us to the danger of generalizing about secularization in a way that is too general to be of use, or alternatively that treats as typical and universal local phenomena that are not universal at all.

Dr. David Martin goes so far as to write: "There is no unitary process called 'secularisation' arising in reaction to a set of characteristics labelled 'religious'. . . . One cannot talk in a unitary way about the causes of secularisation."[3] This might be thought an overstatement, but at least it alerts us to the basic fact that wherever and at whatever rate secularization takes place its features vary according to the cultural and religious background of the community concerned. It simply is not the case that secularization in one community is a carbon copy of secularization in another. Let me illustrate.

Consider three countries belonging to Western Christendom, Germany, France and the United States of America. Germany has a

religious background which is partly Lu-
theran, with a tradition of pietistic religiosity
and subservience to the State, and partly
Roman Catholic, with a tradition of vigorous
political involvement. Against this background, Germany has developed a strong
speculative philosophical tradition mes-
merized by metaphysics, cool towards Christianity, and veering between the cosmic optimism of idealists like Hegel, for whom evil
was good in the making, and the cosmic pessimism of existentialists like Heidegger, for
whom suicide was the only course that made
sense.

In France, by contrast, neither philosophy
nor Protestantism has counted for very much,
but for two centuries French intellectuals
have been on an anticlerical rampage to free
politics, education and social life from the influence of the Roman Catholic Church, which
after being outlawed at the Revolution for its
links with the old regime was reinstated by
Napoleon with financial and other privileges
in 1802, in a settlement which survived into
this century.

In the U.S.A., the dynamics of the religious
situation differ again. "In God We Trust" is
stamped on the coins but religion is shut out
of the schools; a rural, unsophisticated religious culture, Protestant and evangelical,

strongest in the South and Midwest, coexists with a polished humanistic relativism pumped out from centers of learning; and though over 50 percent of Americans belong to and sometimes attend churches, as compared with 10 percent or less practicing their faith in France or England, church links have in America a significance which is much more social and ethnic, and much less religious, than is the case in other places. In each of these three countries today secularization is an observable fact, but in Germany it has sprung from philosophical ideologies, in France from social protest, and in the U.S.A. from a preoccupation with personal achievement, and the details of the process differ in each case.

Now Britain, as is often pointed out, is culturally as well as geographically insular, and so we should expect to find that British secularization too has features that are all its own. My purpose in saying this is simply to underline that, though secularization is a world-wide phenomenon, I shall not in these pages be generalizing about the world, but focusing primarily on Britain, trying to discern as clearly as possible what the secularizing process means here. Similar conditions exist, however, throughout the West—particularly in the U.S.A.—and the lessons learned from the secularization of British society may be profitably applied elsewhere.

8

Before Secularization

In the days before secularization set in—that is, roughly, the early years of this century (later than in France, earlier than in India or Italy)—it used to be affirmed without hesitation that Britain was a Christian country. Certain features of British society could be adduced in support of this claim, features bound up in each case with the Protestant Christianity professed and taught by the two national churches, the Church of England (including at that time Wales), and the Church of Scotland. The main features of this kind were as follows.

1. *A Sense of National Identity and Destiny Under God.*
England had acquired a sense of national religious identity long before the Reformation, through united resistance to the financial and jurisdictionary claims of the Papacy.

During the hundred years which began with the martyring of Protestants under Mary and closed with the setting up of the Commonwealth under Cromwell, there came to be superimposed on the sense of being all together against the Pope a further positive feeling that the Protestant English were a people chosen, like Israel, to enjoy and spread a unique blessedness.[4] England was called to be a model of godliness and a means of good to all nations. This conviction took permanent hold of English minds and found expression two centuries later in the imperial era under Victoria, when it was firmly believed that only cultural and spiritual good could come to any community through being annexed as a British dominion, so that imperial expansion was in truth Britain's service to the world. Similarly, both world wars were widely felt in Britain to be crusades for God against evil. When the jibe is heard, as it still sometimes is, that to the English God is an Englishman, this is part at least of what lies behind it.

2. *A Sense of Unity Between Nation and Church.*

In both England and Scotland the national church was felt to be the nation itself at prayer. This was what the church's established status primarily signified. In England particularly, a certain love-hate relationship between people and church was noticeable at various times after the Restoration. The clergy were often despised for timeserving and money-grabbing, and for inertia, incompetence, and insensitiveness to need; yet the Church of England as such, and the Prayer Book in particular, were held in deep and respectful affection. Both sides of the border people seem to have felt very widely that because they belonged to the nation the well-being of the national church was their concern, even if they rarely or never attended it and had indeed nonconformist attachments. Thus, it was not widely thought incongruous before the twentieth century for Parliament to settle Church affairs, nor did most men take offense at the part played by non-Anglicans in the Parliamentary debates on the revised Prayer Book of 1927-28. The national churches were felt to focus the nation's religious identity in a way that went deeper than any divisions between those churches and their dissenting daughters.

3. *Respect for the Conscience and Rights of Individuals.*
This principle, enshrined in the English common law which grew up in and after

feudal times to guard the rights of those who were not lords or landowners against the claims of those who were, was always felt to have Christian sanction; and similar sanctions prompted and undergirded the establishing of toleration, representative government and constitutional monarchy, and the outlawing of arbitrary courts like Star Chamber, in the seventeenth century. The ultimate reason (so it was maintained) why the law must respect individual rights, liberties and conscientious convictions was that all men were made in the image of God, to live to God and one day to answer to God, and they must not be treated as if their dignity and destiny was less than this. As in Old Testament Israel, so in England, the maintaining of a judicial code which both in legislation and in procedure honored God by honoring his image in man was accepted as a national religious duty.

4. *The Christian Basis of the State.*
"State" means the sum total of legislative, judicial and executive functions whereby a politically autonomous community orders its life. Before the Reformation it was taken for granted that the rulers of those nations that were part of Christendom would govern in a way consonant with Christian faith and

moral ideals, and this was maintained in England after the Reformation without a break, even if the principle was sometimes more honored in the breach than in the observance. The Reformation insistence that magistrates held their power directly from God deepened the sense that government was a stewardship and a form of service to God and man. The Reformers also held explicitly that part of the state's task was to recognize and confirm the distinct authority of the Church in its own sphere, just as the Church must do with the authority of the state, and this concept of partnership whereby Church and state back each other up was maintained by most up until this century.

5. Recognition of Care as a Universal Duty.
The Reformation was a profound spiritual movement, and one of its effects was a tremendous upsurge of private philanthropy and charity.[5] Successive Poor Laws, forerunners of the welfare state, witnessed to the same concern. It came to be part of the national ideal that in a Christian country every citizen, according to his ability, should be a philanthropist—"a good Samaritan," as it has repeatedly been put.

6. Recognition That Public Decency Is a Divine Requirement.
This is a safeguard for purity of heart and a sign of respect for God's image in each other. License of all sorts has of course existed in every age, but public opinion has in the past been strong against it, so that for the most part it has had to keep under cover. There has never yet been a phrase in ordinary English use corresponding to *la dolce vita*.

Such were the main features of "Christian" Britain. If they sound rather old-fashioned when set out like this, that itself is an indication that in recent years British society has changed. We now proceed to consider, first, what caused this change and, second, what it has involved.

9
Why Secularization?

The deepest causes of the de-Christianizing of British society during the past two generations are not peculiar to Britain, but have operated more or less potently all over the Western world. They are well known, for they are often discussed. They may be classified for neatness under the headings of *attraction* (the impact made by appealing alternatives to the Christian view of man), *reaction* (the impact made by the church's failures and inadequacies), and *distraction* (the impact made by practical materialism). Basic to all these factors, however, has been the eclipse first of biblical theism and then of the Bible itself in Western Protestant minds, and it is with this that we must start the story.

In the sixteenth century, at the time of the Reformation, faith in the God who made, sustains and rules this world, and in the Bible as his inspired word of instruction to

man, was clear and strong. Under its influence experimental science was born, as the
reverent study of God's wonderful works.[6] In
the seventeenth and eighteenth centuries,
however, deism, with its idea of the ade-
quacy of natural religion and of God as the
mighty mechanic who, having set the world
going, is now content to be its absentee land-
lord, had the effect of undermining belief in
both special providence and special revelation; it barred God out of his world, and si-
lenced him into the bargain. Kant's *Religion
Within the Bounds of Pure Reason* (1793), which
reduces religion to performing moral duties
viewed as God's commands, shows this
tendency at its height.

Nineteenth-century German idealist philosophy restored the sense of God's nearness
which deism had destroyed, but it was only a
case of out of the frying pan into the fire.
Idealists saw knowledge of God as an aspect
of self-consciousness, and equated God with
our thoughts and feelings about him, and
denied just as firmly as the deists had done
that God reveals, by some process other than
philosophic reflection, things that have not
entered into the heart of philosophic man.
The Bible was seen as a record of religion
rather than of revelation, and biblical criti-
cism was practiced in a way which convinced

onlookers that the Bible could not be trusted about anything, while physical science, working with an interpretative model of evolutionary development and making great strides in all fields, was thought to have exposed the biblical view of God and the world as primitive and in no sense scientific.

After the First World War theism revived a little in the West and the sophistry of the supposition that science has refuted, or could refute, the biblical view of God's relation to this world began to be seen by one and another. But the damage was already done; the course of Western intellectual development was now set in a non-Christian direction, and when the war of 1914-18 knocked the bottom out of the optimistic evolutionary view of man as getting better and better it was to the atheistic optimism of the communists and the atheistic pessimism of Freud and existentialism that men turned. In Britain it was Freudianism that had most influence.

Freud was a determinist, halfway to being a behaviorist; he saw each man as driven by irrational impulses of which he was largely unconscious, and which he repressed to his own ruin. Freud saw religion as a neurosis, God being the personified projection of a tyrannical conscience (the super-ego) which was itself the neurotic product of repressed jealousy towards one's father (the Oedipus complex).

It is relevant when weighing this idea to bear in mind that in clinical practice Freud had found some cases of infantile jealousy of fathers, and also that he was himself an atheist Jew in an uneasy relationship with his own father. His prescription for mental health was to let repressed desires come out, particularly in the matter of sex; his prescription for society was tight restraints to prevent aggressive desires destroying civilized life altogether. This seemed pleasant good sense to many people in the dispirited days between the two world wars, and the Freudian view of life was widely taken up as a credible alternative to what was felt to be the incredible, indeed superstitious view held by Christians, which in any case (so it was held) Freudianism could explain away.

The de-Christianizing process was further helped by the contempt, mild or fierce, that the Church's inertia in the face of change provoked in the popular mind. Part of the problem here has been the static way of thinking which stemmed from the so-called "medieval synthesis" of religion and all life which was the scholastic theologians' supreme achievement. "The trouble about the mediaeval synthesis," wrote F. R. Barry, "was that it was far too complete. The Church and Christianity were equated with a temporary historical situation and a transient phase in cultural evolution, assuming that it was final and permanent. For example, the social ethic of St. Thomas takes for granted a small-town economy, and is viable only in that context. . . . Theologies built on the doctrine of the 'natural law' tend to a static social philosophy, and tend to forget that history means change. . . . But to resist change is to be destroyed by change. . . ." Under the pressure of the widening interests, new social patterns, explorations of individuality, and new sense of history that flowed from the Renaissance, "increasingly wide areas of life began to assert their independence from 'religious' or churchly control, and more and more 'secular,' this-worldly interests began to claim and vindicate their autonomy. . . ."[7]

This is a generalization about several centuries of European history, but something of this kind certainly took place in England, in its own very English way. Hooker's *Laws of Ecclesiastical Polity* was a late sixteenth-century defense of the Anglican establishment built on foundations of "natural law"; it assumed an absolute monarchy and a single church structure to which the whole nation belonged. It remained the standard apologia for the Church of England up to the First World War, two centuries after it first went out of date on both these latter points. As nineteenth-century men came to see more and more clearly that industrial and urbanized patterns of life had come to stay, so indignation at the Church of England's rural and reactionary mentality increased, and progressive persons turned away in disgust, dismissing the Church, and Christianity with it, as an obstructive irrelevance. It is to be feared that during the past century there have been many for whom the conservatism of the Church has undermined the credibility of the faith.

As for the distraction of materialism, the pressure point for British people seems not to be so much theoretical (whether Christianity is true) as practical (whether worship and spiritual life matter). The feeling has spread that the good life for man in God's world is to avail himself of the endless enjoyments which technology now puts at his disposal, and that it is not important to take time and trouble learning to know and serve God, since God will accept us all, whether we have loved him or not. If we cannot be accepted for actually being good, we shall at least be accepted for not doing so badly as we might have done.

Alistair MacIntyre's famous description of the Englishman's creed as a belief that there is no God, and it is wise to pray to him from time to time, is as false as it is clever; it is the exact opposite of the truth. Various sociological investigations during the past thirty years have made it clear that most Englishmen still possess a residual belief in "one above," however vaguely conceived. F. R. Barry quotes "the immortal remark" (made to him?): "After all, bishop, I suppose we all believe in a sort of a something"[8]—yet most Englishmen neither attend a church, nor relate their belief to matters of personal morality, nor regularly pray. Atheists—that is, persons who deny the Christian faith because they deny the existence of the personal God of Christian theism—are a minority, but practical atheism—that is, living as if theoretical atheism were true—is the life style of the great mass of our people.

The term "secularism" was coined by G. J. Holyoake in a fine flush of Victorian indignation to mean "the doctrine that morality should be based on regard to the well-being of mankind in the present life, to the exclusion of all considerations drawn from belief in God or a future state." According to the *Oxford Dictionary of the Christian Church*, it is now used "in a more general sense for the modern tendency to ignore, if not to deny, the principles of supernatural religion in the interpretation of the world and existence."

It is all too apt a description of the current British outlook. What has caused this? Not so much dogmatic unbelief, it would seem, as on the one hand a sense that the Church, the official instructor in Christianity, is remote from real life, and on the other hand a clamor, never-ending, from the manufacturers, the media and the automobile—"buy this"; "stop, look and listen to that"; "move around, and go somewhere else"—a clamor which drowns the quieter voices suggesting that time should be given to exploring eternal issues.

Materialism in Britain operates less as an argument than as an enchantment. It is not theoretical but pragmatic, calling for and capturing not so much men's assent as their attention. Its motivating force is not hostility to the truth but rather love of the world, which drives out every other concern. Like all other modes of sin, the more worldly mindedness is indulged the stronger it grows. The present degree of secularism in our society is of itself a strong force pressing for secularization to be carried further.

10
Secularization in Practice

The secularization of British national life is a complex process of which you and I, willy-nilly, are part, and to focus it for study is not easy. The following factors, however, are certainly major elements in what is going on.

1. *A Drift From the Churches.*
Apart from some well-heeled white-collar suburban areas and some nondormitory villages of the Ambridge type, this drift is countrywide, though it is more pronounced in England and Wales than in Scotland. In many working-class population areas, "drift" would be the wrong word, for people there have never been churchgoers since the first houses were put up—often more than a hundred years ago. As today people who move to new housing estates and high-rise flats often lose any churchgoing habits they had before, so it was in the early days of the

Industrial Revolution when families moved from the country to work in factories and mills.

The nonavailability of churches has sometimes been blamed for this, but it was due more perhaps to the pressures and claims of the industrial way of life. There are still very few blue-collar industrial workers in the Protestant churches, which in view of the present size of our industrial population— something over half the country's total work force—is a daunting fact indeed. In this century, though the total population of Britain has increased by more than half, all indigenous Protestant bodies, including the two national churches, have been in decline numerically so far as active membership is concerned, and the Roman Catholic Church seems to maintain its strength only through immigration. Whereas on a Sunday in 1851, when an unofficial census was taken, one in three Englishmen went to a place of worship (a proportion which at the time was felt to be terribly low), the number on an ordinary Sunday in 1974 is no higher than one in seven and is more likely to approximate to one in ten or twelve.[9]

2. *A Drift From Christian Knowledge.*
Whether there is less real, as distinct from

formal, Christianity in Britain today than there was fifty or a hundred years ago is something which only God knows. But many have observed that, whereas until recently most people carried with them a smattering of Bible knowledge, the young people of today reveal by and large a striking lack of such knowledge. While more popular Christian books are produced, bought and presumably read in Britain today than ever before, and while the Bible holds its place among the bestsellers, the circle touched by Christian literature does not seem to enlarge much, if at all. Outside this circle public interest in Christianity has sunk to such a low ebb that casual knowledge about it no longer brushes off on the uncommitted in the way that it once did, and in the way that casual knowledge about, say, pop singers and the football leagues brushes off today on people who have no personal interest in either. Christianity has ceased to be a matter of general knowledge and become a private concern which those whose interest is not caught up by it just ignore.

3. *A Shift From Public Christian Commitment.*
We are moving from the ethos of a Christian state and society to the ethos of its secular counterpart. What this means may be seen

from two small books, T. S. Eliot's *The Idea of a Christian Society* (1939) and D. L. Munby's *The Idea of a Secular Society* (1963).

Eliot sought to revive the ideal of "Christendom" in a modern context. Defining a Christian society as a community of "men whose Christianity is communal before being individual,"[10] he looked for a Christian elite (a "clerisy," that is, a body of committed churchmen, ordained and lay) who would penetrate society at every level and leave no area of life without its ideological guardians. "The clerisy he intended, somewhat like a social class, or more precisely an intellectual class, a meritocracy," writes Leslie Paul, "would share not so much a common political programme as common (Christian) values and creeds and a common feeling for the dimensions of the sacred in the secular world."[11] They would leaven the social lump to the extent of maintaining a Christian public opinion and a general readiness publicly to uphold Christian standards.

Munby wrote against this, protesting that nowadays such an ideal is not merely impractical but actually undesirable, and that the goal for Christians to aim at is rather that of a secular society founded on respect for the variety of individuals and therefore on tolerance for all views which are not in a direct way socially disruptive. Here is Lesslie New-bigin's summary of the six features which according to Munby will mark such a society:

"(i) It 'refuses to commit itself as a whole to any particular view of the nature of the universe and of the place of man in it.' In such a society the views of atheists and of Christians will be equally respected, and will be given equal opportunity to influence education, broadcasting and other aspects of public life. Such a society will therefore not approve any state recognition of religion.

"(ii) A secular society will be a pluralist society in the sense that it will not enforce (whether by social pressure or state regulation) 'a uniform attitude in important matters of human behaviour and values.' It will thus accept the fact that education 'will be as much a sphere of divided beliefs and cultures as any other realm of life.

"(iii) A secular society will be a tolerant society. It will . . . give the benefit of the doubt to deviant belief and conduct.

"(iv) The organisations and institutions of a secular society will have strictly limited aims," (namely, to provide facilities without giving directives). . . . "A secular society deflates the pretensions of politicians and judges to be leaders of society or 'prophet-priests of the national conscience.' " (Any such pretensions on the part of Christians were ruled out earlier, under (i)).

"(v) A secular society will solve its problems by collecting and analysing the relevant facts so that people may be able to make rationally the decisions necessary to enable them to achieve their desires; it will not try to tell people what their desires ought to be.

"(vi) A secular society will be a society without 'official images.' 'If there are no common aims, there cannot be a common set of images reflecting the common ideals and emotions of everyone. Nor can there be any common ideal types of behaviour for universal application.' "[12]

Munby's pipe dream is vulnerable from several standpoints. First, if practicability is the issue, it is impracticable in a much profounder sense than Eliot's; for whereas Eliot's problem would be simply to find enough Christians who have got what it takes to fulfil his aims, Munby's problem would be to find a way of holding together a society which has no unifying or motivating goal and no agreed moral basis save the one belief that centrifugal individuality should be given its head. But to enthrone so socially disintegrative a belief to be the principle of society's cohesion would be a guarantee of social disaster. Has Munby not heard of original sin, nor learned from the Bible and world history what happens when every man does what is right in his own eyes?

Moreover, nature abhors an ideological vacuum no less than a physical one, and history suggests that the morally unqualified tolerance which Munby seems to want, and which some have seen as one dimension of decadence,[13] will sooner or later produce by reaction some kind of ideological dictatorship, which will be accepted with hardly a struggle because men will feel that any unitive communal goal is better than none.

Second, Munby seems to have hold of the wrong end of his own stick; as David Edwards points out, what his arguments really defend is "not the 'secular society' but the 'pluralist' or 'open' society. On Mr. Munby's showing the *state*, not the society, needs to be secular."[14]

Third, the biblical insistence that all life and all power, including political power, is from God and for God surely obliges Christians to seek a society in which the true God is acknowledged, and approved standards come as close as possible to the behavior pattern that God has prescribed as being both pleasing to him and beneficial to us. To settle for a society which has no standards save unlimited tolerance is not to love one's neighbor, but to fail to love him. To secure his right to reject the Christian way if he feels he must is indeed a Christian duty (Munby is correct there), but to work for (rather than strive against) a state of affairs which will make that rejection easier, by taking from Christianity all its present backing in public opinion (which is what Munby's preferred option really amounts to), would be a betrayal of both God and man.

But we must rein in our horses. The purpose of reviewing Eliot and Munby was not to make a case for one view against the other, but to clarify our understanding of what a public Christian commitment, or lack of it, involves, as a preparation for trying to estimate how far the public Christian commitment of former days has been given up in our present-day British society; and to this we must now briefly turn.

Have we a secular state in Britain? Yes and no. As early as 1913, when the English state was definitely "Church of England" and Free Churchmen were still seen as lapsed Anglicans, J. N. Figgis argued, in *The Churches and the Modern State*, that the state's task was to "hold the ring" for all churches, securing their legal protection and freedom to function but not committing itself to any one of them. Though the formalities of the Establishment remain, the state today has in practice moved nearer to Figgis's recommended position.

Under synodical government Parliament is not now asked, nor would it any longer be willing, to settle the affairs of the Church of England (though this is only to say that the two national churches, north and south of the border, are now in practice on a par at this point). Bishops still speak as representative churchmen in the House of Lords, but Christian principles and Church opinion seem to have little or no effect on legislative programs. Yet the state is not anti-Christian or anti-Church in any active way, as it is for instance in communist countries. Though maintaining a formally uncommitted stance, it may fairly be described as still a fellow traveller with the Church. In education, broadcasting and television a measure of Christian privilege still remains, and the part played by the Church on ceremonial occasions (providing official chaplaincies, leading in prayer and worship, and so on) is still evidently welcomed.

"Surveys of public opinion," wrote David Edwards in 1969, "show that the privileges are not in fact widely resented. The great majority of English parents seem to want religious worship and instruction in schools, and religious broadcasts have large audience. . . . Some evidence that the British people wishes to observe high standards of decency and compassion comes in its acceptance of the legal prohibition of public prostitution and racial discrimination."[15]

All this seems still to be true. Public appeal to our Christian heritage can still be made, though modern politicians usually leave it to others to make it. The welfare state embodies recognizably Christian ideals of care, and recognizably Christian ideals of respect for the rights and conscience of the individual, plus the traditional Christian scheme of social values still animate the British judicial system. Thus it would seem that the British state, though secularized to a degree, is not yet wholly secular; more of its Christian roots remain than might at first be thought.

Have we, then, a secular society on our hands? Again no categorical answer can be given. On the debit side, it is clear that in matters of personal morality—honesty, sexual restraint, fidelity, thrift, self-control, public spiritedness, responsible gratitude, and such things—a great deal of the Christian tradition of teaching, and the public opinion that went with it, has been eroded, so that there are many young Britons today to whom it has simply never occurred, nor ever been seriously suggested, that the practice of these virtues might be part of the good life.

Statistics show that crime (especially crimes of violence), illegitimacy and venereal disease, drug offenses and outlay on gambling (not to mention tobacco, drink or installment buying), are increasing all the time: though in America these things are worse. Also, a great deal of dehumanizing thought about personal life (sometimes called humanist, sometimes not) has been pumped out, and has presumably made some converts, in recent years. It is notable, however, that when Os Guinness set out to analyze this array of ideas (in *The Dust of Death*, 1973) he went for most of his examples to America and continental Europe, where the ideas have been developed in more radical and forceful ways than here.

Similarly, the current revival of interest in the occult among those on whom Christianity has no hold (a predictable development, since nature abhors a religious vacuum no less than any other sort) is a sad sign, no doubt, but there is more of it in some other countries. Leslie Paul has solid warrant for his generalization about the pessimistic, nihilistic trend of modern literature— "whatever the philosophies and ideologies say, literature testifies that man seeks in vain, outside his moments of orgasm, for meaning, hope, or identity"[16]—yet it is again notable that his most striking evidence for this thesis comes from writers outside Britain. On the credit side, it is clear that Britain has still a very potent legacy of Christian ethical ideals for personal conduct, often linked with a continuing belief, however misshapen, in God and in the ultimate significance of morality.

The conclusion seems to be that though no public Christian commitment now marks our society we have not yet sunk so deep into the post-Christian void as some other communities have done. In the world of ideas, strongly anti-Christian currents run; but the British people in general do not take them with full seriousness. What will happen tomorrow nobody knows, but this seems to be where we are today.

4. *A Detaching of Moral Values From Their Anchorage in Christian Faith.*
What we see today is a secularizing of ethics. This is the other side of the picture sketched in the last two paragraphs. Certainly, Christian moral attitudes and behavior patterns still survive in circles where Christian faith is no longer present to give them sanction; but how long can they last under those conditions? High-minded humanists who value

the Christian code of loving one's neighbor think it can last indefinitely on its own merits, because (they say) it clearly makes for human happiness. Christians wonder if this is not too starry-eyed. How long will a sense of human dignity survive after man's creation in God's image has been forgotten? Or a spirit of care and mutual service survive among men who forget the obligation to serve God? How long before Christian toleration, which was based on respect for God's image in man, will turn, as in some quarters it is already doing, into a total permissiveness based simply on hedonism—"living for kicks"? How soon will our heritage of Christian ideological capital run out? How long will God's common grace restrain sin in a community that has given up the faith in him that it once professed? In the Bible, self-destruction through lawless self-indulgence is one form of divine judgment on erring communities: may this be what we now face?[17] These questions are easier to ask than to answer: but it is at least clear that while Christian morality, personal and social, lacks the sanctions of Christian faith it is constantly at risk.

11
Evaluating Secularization

The process which has been described above in its British form, and which currently operates, with local variations, throughout the Western world, has been variously evaluated by theologians. At one extreme stands Harvey Cox, who in *The Secular City* (1965) maintained that urban secularization is to be seen as a wholly good and Christian development, even though one of its by-products is that God has become anonymous and is no longer known. Others from an opposite extreme have denounced secularization as unmixed apostasy. It is not possible here to enter into the complexities of this debate: I limit myself in this final section to making four "perspectival" points which may help to shape our overall response to what we see happening around us.

First, *the secularizing of society was inevitable*. Whether we applaud it as "man come of age" or deplore it as man off the rails, we should recognize that the secularization of Christendom was something that sooner or later had to happen, and any nostalgic idea that it could have been avoided should be banished from our minds. For Christendom, both unreformed (in the Middle Ages) and reformed (in the sixteenth and seventeenth centuries) was a Church-dominated, rural and static culture, prescientific, preindustrial and pretechnological, full of fanciful ideas about nature, man and the cosmos, and quite unprepared for rapid social change. From the Renaissance there flowed, like a river growing in size and speed, first the knowledge explosion and then the technological explosion. This was the biggest cultural trauma in Western history so far, and it made Christendom's historic way of thinking about life under God seem increasingly remote.

I do not imply that the Christendom synthesis of knowledge and culture informed and interpreted by biblical faith cannot be successfully rethought and realized afresh in our time—with T. S. Eliot, John Baillie, Herman Dooyeweerd, Francis Schaeffer and many more I think it can. But it would have been unrealistic to expect that the West could work through this trauma of transition without great numbers of people throwing out the baby of Christian faith with the bathwater of Christendom's prescientific outlook because they thought that the two were one. So we ought not to panic, as if we face something enigmatic and inexplicable, when we find that this has actually taken place.

Second, *the secularizing of society has brought real spiritual loss.* Against those who hail secularization as if it were God's kingdom coming, the sad side of the process—the "expense of spirit," to use Shakespeare's phrase, and the eternal ruin of souls—must be stressed. When individuals or groups who once professed the faith give it up, it is apostasy, a falling away; and the end of apostasy, as the Epistle to the Hebrews declares, is death, in every sense of that word (see 6:4-8, 10:26-31). By the light of the Bible we recognize in the process that has been going on throughout Europe for two centuries, and intensively in England for two generations, the pattern of spiritual decline spelled out in Romans 1:20-32 where Paul describes how men transfer their instinct to worship and serve from the true God to things they have made themselves, and how this loss of God leads to the loss of good in human relations, and an increasingly frenzied descent into debauchery, all provoking divine judgment.

Inevitable as the secularizing of the West

may have been, that does not excuse the apostasy which is bound up with it; and without questioning God's lordship over the process we must recognize the reality of his wrath against the spiritual decline which it has brought. Jeremiah (9:1) wished that his head were waters, and his eyes a fountain of tears, that he might weep for his people: anyone with an ounce of compassion in him will feel the same as he looks at the tokens of the spiritual state of Britain today.

Third, *the secularizing of society tends to disintegrate society.* The fact must be faced that many current social trends lead towards nihilism and anarchy. True as it may be that we are still distant from both, and other communities are perhaps nearer, it is to this and nowhere else that the road we are following leads. The seeds of all kinds of sin lie in every human heart; restraints of law, custom, religion and public opinion may hold them in check; but the more these restraints are weakened, the more we may expect to see these seeds grow, and human relations in society being disrupted as a result. That the restraint of religion is being weakened seems clear from the decline of the churches and the general withering of religion in the home. That other restraints are being progressively weakened seems to follow from contemporary willingness to tolerate what earlier eras would have thought intolerable—a state of moral apathy which we call the permissive society.

The weakening process may be expected to continue, for permissiveness has a continually erosive effect. Public blasphemy recoils on the community which tolerates it by eroding the capacity to respect or hold sacred anything at all. Pornography recoils similarly by dehumanizing our thoughts about sex, and so dehumanizing those who think them. Violence glorified by artists and the media as a way of establishing individuality in a hostile world dulls the inner sensibilities which ordinarily hold back the rage that lies hid in all our hearts, and so tends to brutalize and leads us step by step towards the jungle. The society which tolerates these things and has no strong public opinion against them is terribly vulnerable. I was once in a boat which began drifting towards an open dam, and I remember how I felt as it began to pick up speed, before we got it under control. Watching British society move during the past decade has often given me similar feelings.

In the early eighteenth century, as J. Wesley Bready showed in *England: Before and After Wesley*, English society underwent a decline into brutalized irreligion and immorality that bade fair to produce total social chaos had it not been arrested. What put that process into reverse for a century and a half was the impetus towards personal and social regeneration that sprang from the Evangelical Revival. Bready's view of the social dynamics of the Revival followed that of Elie Halévy, who had written: "In the vast work of social organisation which is one of the dominant characteristics of nineteenth-century England it would be difficult to over-estimate the part played by the Wesleyan revival. . . . We shall explain by this movement . . . what we may truly term the miracle of modern England, anarchist but orderly, practical and businesslike, but religious and even pietist."[18]

Historical parallels are always in danger of oversimplifying problems, but they can sometimes suggest solutions. It may be that today as in the eighteenth-century spiritual revival can save our society from further dehumanization and collapse. It is certainly hard to see, in the long run, what else can. These things should drive Christians to their knees.

Fourth, *the secularizing of society is a summons to Christian action*. Jesus' disciples are called to be the salt of the earth, the working antiseptic factor that keeps society from decay. So Christians should use whatever power and influence they have in the social system to set up and safeguard public righteousness, and to further decisions which express Christian values. Part of the task facing every Christian generation is to see how far society can in this way be "Christianized." This follows from the "cultural mandate" of Genesis 1:28, linked with God's concern for community holiness as expressed by the Mosaic law and the prophets, and with Jesus' call to neighbor-love; and it follows equally from Jesus' directive to worldwide evangelism in Matthew 28:19, for the establishing of Christian patterns of community is itself a help and a step forward in making disciples.

If, therefore, Christians lack power to exert Christianizing influence, they should consider before God how they might acquire it; and if no access to power seems open to them, they should still seek, as did the company of evangelical leaders to which Wesley belonged, to create alternative patterns of communal living in homes, extended families, local churches and ad hoc "task force" associations which will function in society as a city set on a hill, demonstrating to the world around the power of Christ in action.

In any case, Christians owe it to God and

their fellow men and women to maintain constantly that the divine moral law is not only obligatory but also natural in the sense of constituting the only ethical fuel on which human nature can run without burning itself up. Human nature at bottom does not change, whatever cultural shifts occur at surface level, and it remains as true as it ever was that joy and fulfilment are only found within the framework for conduct that God's law—his *torah*, that is, his fatherly instruction—erects. And Christians need also to proclaim with new energy that the living Lord Jesus, the Christ of Calvary, of the Emmaus Road and of the upper room, is the sole source and secret of freedom and meaning for man, just as they must display in their own lives the contentment which comes of having found this secret and knowing that it is theirs for ever.

Most of all, Christians should labor to understand the secularization that goes on around them—what arguments and hurts (usually the latter rather than the former) lead people to embrace secularism, what issues hold their attention, why their way of seeking true community and true individuality is counterproductive, and how an active Christian minority (which is all we can hope for at present) can take up the problems of a drifting society, neither denying nor oversimplifying them, but irradiating them with the light of biblical truth and the reality of divine grace.

It is time to seek the Lord, and to do some homework.

Questions for Thought and Discussion

1. What is good, and what is bad, about the current secularization of our society?
2. How far do the attitudes of the organized Church today contribute to its eclipse as an influence in society?
3. Is the ideal of a Christian society realistic today in any form?
4. Is it possible to justify the attempts of Christians to bring public life into line with God's law when they themselves are a minority group?

Notes

[1] Bryan Wilson, *Religion in Secular Society* (Harmondsworth: Pelican ed., 1969), p. 14; compare David Edwards, *Religion and Change* (London: Hodder and Stoughton, 1969), p. 16: "Secularisation occurs when supernatural religion—that is, religion based on 'belief in God or a future state'—becomes private, optional and problematic."

[2] Lesslie Newbigin, *Honest Religion for Secular Man* (London: SCM, 1966), pp. 15f.

[3] David Martin, "Towards Eliminating the Concept of Secularisation," *Penguin Survey of the Social Sciences* (Harmondsworth: Penguin, 1965), p. 176. Martin wants to see the term dropped, as scientifically bogus and loaded, "a tool of counter-religious

ideologies," *The Religious and the Secular* (London: Routledge and Kegan Paul, 1969), p. 9.

[4]See W. Haller, *Foxe's Book of Martyrs and the Elect Nation* (London: Cape, 1963).

[5]See W. K. Jordon, *Philanthropy in England, 1480-1660* (London: Allen and Unwin, 1959).

[6]See R. Hooykaas, *Religion and the Rise of Modern Science* (Edinburgh: Scottish Academic Press, 1972).

[7]F. R. Barry, *Secular and Supernatural* (London: SCM, 1969), pp. 40f.

[8]*op. cit.*, p. 22, note 22.

[9]For some statistics, see David Martin, *A Sociology of English Religion*, chapters 2, 3 (London: SCM, 1967), and Bryan Wilson, *op. cit.*, chapter 1. Most recently, the *U.K. Protestant Missions Handbook, Vol. 2 Home* (London: Evangelical Alliance, 1977) gives 182 per 1000 on an average Sunday (p. 5), but it has been suggested that this may include children at Sunday School.

[10]T. S. Eliot, *The Idea of a Christian Society* (London: Faber, 1939), p. 19.

[11]Leslie Paul, *Alternatives to Christian Belief* (London: Hodder and Stoughton, 1967), pp. 6f.

[12]Newbigin, *op. cit.* pp. 126f.

[13]Compare C. E. M. Joad, *Decadence* (London: Faber, 1948). Joad finds the essence of decadence "in the view that experience is valuable or is at least to be valued for its own sake, irrespective of the quality or kind of the experience, and in the appropriate beliefs about life, morals, art and society which entail and are entailed by this view, together with the scales of value and modes of taste associated with these beliefs" (p. 95).

[14]Edwards, *op. cit.* p. 99.

[15]*op cit.*, p. 98. For evidence about religious education, see P. May and O. R. Johnston, *Religion in our Schools* (London: Hodder and Stoughton, 1968).

[16]Paul, *op cit.*, pp. 182 f. For parallel evidence from the world of art, see H. R. Rookmaaker, *Modern Art and the Death of a Culture* (London: IVP, 1970).

[17]"Our Western world has not been faithful to its Christian inheritance. Its values have too often been those of materialism, pleasure and luxury. It has lost the virtues of simplicity of life. Its morals have fallen far short of the righteousness of Christ. It has been complacent about the existence of terrible poverty and hunger in many parts of the world. Is it surprising if the judgment

of God falls upon us?" (A. M. Ramsey, Archbishop of Canterbury, *Diocesan Notes*, January 1974).

[18]Cited from J. Wesley Bready, *England: Before and After Wesley* (London: Hodder and Stoughton, 3rd impression, 1939), pp. 179f.

FOR FURTHER READING

Books mentioned in the text and notes, and also:

Baillie, John. *What Is Christian Civilization?* New York: Charles Scribner's Sons, 1945.

Barbour, Ian G. *Issues in Science and Religion.* New York: Harper & Row, 1971.

Blamires, Henry. *The Christian Mind.* Ann Arbor, Mich.: Servant Publications, 1978.

Casserley, J. V. Langmead. *The Retreat From Christianity in the Modern World.* London: Longmans, Green & Co., 1952.

Chadwick, Owen. *The Secularization of the European Mind in the Nineteenth Century.* New York: Cambridge University Press, 1976.

Heller, Erich. *The Disinherited Mind.* New York: Harcourt Brace Jovanovich, 1975.

Hill, Michael. *The Sociology of Religion*. New York: Basic Books, 1973.

Jeeves, Malcolm A. *The Scientific Enterprise and Christian Faith*. Downers Grove, Ill.: InterVarsity Press, 1969.

Lewis, C. S. *The Abolition of Man*. New York: Macmillan Co., 1967.

————. *The Pilgrim's Regress*. Grand Rapids, Mich.: Eerdmans, 1975.

Mascall, E. L. *The Secularization of Christianity*. New York: Holt, Rinehart & Winston, 1966.

Pornography: The Longford Report. London: Coronet Books, 1972.

Schaeffer, Francis A. *The Church at the End of the Twentieth Century*. Downers Grove, Ill.: InterVarsity Press, 1970.

————. *The God Who Is There*. Downers Grove, Ill.: InterVarsity, 1968.

Wickham, E. R. *Church and People in an Industrial City*. London: Lutterworth Press, 1957.